ARCTURUS

ARCTURUS

This edition published in 2014 by
Arcturus Publishing Limited
26/27 Bickels Yard, 151–153 Bermondsey Street,
London SE1 3HA

Copyright © 2013 Arcturus Publishing Limited

ISBN: 978-1-78212-886-1
AD003954UK

Printed in China

Contents

All photographs from **Getty Images** apart from those below:
Mary Evans (52, 120); **Corbis** (132-133, 138-139, 142);
Topfoto (14-15, 36-37, 50, 54-55, 63, 80-81, 84)

Introduction

• •

As the old joke goes, if you can remember the Sixties you weren't there. The image of a decade lost in a haze of mind-expanding drugs and love-ins is one that has endured, yet most people don't remember it like that at all. Whether you remember it or not, the good news is that it was recorded more comprehensively than any decade before, in print and on celluloid, on television and in movies, in music and in poetry. This book is a collection of fascinating photographs that capture the Sixties in all its many guises, captioned with recollections that draw from the record of the time and bring those vibrant days back to life.

The air of revolution – cultural, youthful, sexual and political – that pervaded the Sixties was fomented in the latter years of the previous decade, when the post-war rebuilding of Britain was bearing fruit, people were tasting freedom like never before and they wanted more of it. The Sixties took that attitude and developed it into a succession of 'movements', each of which had the power to captivate and shock in equal measure. And it was a time to take sides. Were you a Mod? A Rocker? A Hippie? Some people managed to be all three. Were you into The Beatles or The Stones? You tuned your tranny to Radio Luxembourg or one of the other pirate radio stations and picked up your musical education from across the waves.

It was a time of major political upheaval. Britain lost Sir Winston Churchill in

1965, America lost JFK two years before. There was Vietnam, Fidel Castro and the Cuban missile crisis, the Cold War and the Campaign for Nuclear Disarmament. Young people became politically active, pop music and poetry took up the call for peace and the weapon of choice became the flower.

Each movement and each new idea had its own style and Britain became the global centre for fashion, with Carnaby Street at its epicentre. Mini skirts, parkas, Chelsea boots and kaftans all played their part in creating the look. Boys grew their hair long, girls cut theirs short and parents complained that they couldn't tell the difference any more.

The spirit of invention was still very much alive. The Sixties introduced us to the audio cassette and the video recorder, Action Man and today's version of Lego, supermarkets, motorways and heart transplants, the hovercraft, ice cream vans and Concorde. People 'backed Britain', the flags came out for Princess Margaret, the England football team and Manchester United and from 1968 the clocks stayed forward, making those long winter evenings just a shade lighter. Not that it mattered; there were plenty of reasons to stay indoors: three television channels, colour TV, *Coronation Street* and *Doctor Who* and the new hero on the big screen was James Bond.

Though the decade ended with dropouts, dissolution and disharmony, the Sixties remains arguably the most memorable decade of all time – a time when style, energy and passion were given free rein.

The Sixties was the decade when youth came to the fore and parents were encouraged to pay more consideration to their children's feelings and not to 'criticise what you can't understand'. In the main,

The Kids Are Alright

though, children were still expected to do what they were told, to respect authority and to be polite. The innocence of youth was still mostly intact though there were a few hints of rebellion creeping in, mostly expressed in the length of your hair.

The way children played was going through an upheaval. The streets where groups of children had traditionally gathered were being taken over by cars, or the houses demolished and replaced by high-rise flats and communal playgrounds where nobody really felt much at home.

But there were lots of new machines to get excited about: fancy cars and motorbikes, jet planes and space rockets. Boys wanted to be a spaceman, girls wanted to marry one, unless he was one of those aliens you saw on *Doctor Who*, the ones that sent you scurrying to hide behind the sofa.

In 1961 Britons discovered that they owned a remote volcanic island in the South Atlantic called Tristan da Cunha. What brought this to their attention was a volcanic eruption, which resulted in the 200 or so inhabitants, of whom these are two, taking refuge in England for a couple of years.

Ten-pin bowling was the new fad of the Sixties, with the first alleys opening in 1960. People were bowled over by the clever automatic pinsetters and the tracks that fetched the balls back for you, but there was no electronic scoring – that had to be done with pen and paper.

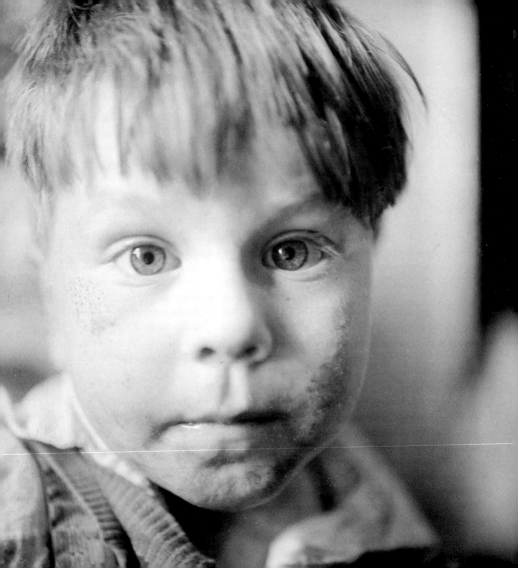

Left *Harold Macmillan's assertion at the end of the Fifties that people had 'never had it so good' didn't apply to everyone. Many still lived in slums with no hot water or electricity, and children like this boy from Wapping showed there was much to do before everybody could enjoy a decent standard. of living.*

Above *The Twist was here and the Mashed Potato was coming, but the close dancing routines of the ballroom were still ingrained in the wider culture and were learned from a young age. This little girl is either trying to teach her partner to waltz or is about to throw him over her shoulder.*

IN THE COUNTRY *Shoes with buckles, shorts with braces, hair that came over your ears and a drive to the countryside in an open-top car – summer in the Sixties brought the heady perfume of freedom, though all you cared about as a child was that the sun was shining and there was grass to run around on.*

Left *The 'I'm Backing Britain' campaign was launched in 1968 in an attempt to boost the economy by encouraging everyone to work an extra half day for free. With the Union Jack as its emblem, the campaign tapped into the people's patriotic fervour but was ultimately unsuccessful, an outcome that this little girl has clearly foreseen.*

Right *The golden age of fashion photography was under way and there was no shortage of aspiring models, eager to take their place in front of the lens. It was also a golden age for advertising and children were often used to sell new household goods like washing powder.*

A STITCH IN TIME *Blackpool? Margate? No, it's the banks of the River Thames by Tower Bridge, where you could go to play on the sand and enjoy the sunshine, under the watchful eye of a 'beach attendant' who ensured safety and performed useful tasks like sewing up tears in boys' trousers.*

Food glorious food
· ·

Dinner time in the Sixties became a much more varied and generally more exciting occasion for children. The traditional meat and two veg was still considered the healthy option for a growing lad, and fish and chips was still the nation's favourite dish, but mums were finding more convenient ways to feed the kids quickly and easily. You could buy all sorts of frozen food, such as fish fingers, chips and peas, and tinned fruit and vegetables were popular. Tinned baked beans were all the rage, helped by the catchy slogan 'Beanz Meanz Heinz' and pudding might consist of tinned peaches or pears with a dollop of ice cream. Yum.

Mum had much more choice when she went shopping (it was still generally mum who did the food shopping). The new supermarkets allowed her to help herself to an array of goods from exotic corners of the world and the concept of seasonality was beginning to go out of the window. Now she could buy tomatoes in December and put them in a salad with one of those funny avocado things.

THE MARTIANS ARE COMING! *Space became the new frontier in the Sixties and with the exploits of Yuri Gagarin, Neil Armstrong et al. came a fascination for extra-terrestrial aliens. Doctor Who fuelled the obsession through his weekly tussles with the Daleks, Cybermen and other monsters on television and the decade ended with Davie Bowie's* Space Oddity.

Above *Everyone aspired to owning their own car and the toys of the day reflected the growing obsession with life on four wheels. Pushing the thing was the hard part, so you often ended up just parking and having a chat with passers-by, while leaning casually on the steering wheel.*

Right *The joy of having a car of your own rarely had anything to do with taking it out for a drive. It was caring for the vehicle that really appealed: the cleaning, the maintenance and the repair. Now you could be like dad and spend all your spare time underneath the car cursing.*

White wedding

••••••••••••••••••••••••

Bridesmaids and pageboys gather themselves for a traditional white wedding at a church in London. In the Sixties, if you met someone and wanted to live with them, you generally got married. Only about one per cent of people under the age of 50 lived with their partners without being married and they tended to be regarded with disapproval by mainstream society. Most marriages took place in church too. More than half of the population regularly attended church and when it came to tying the knot, more than two-thirds of marriages took place in church. In most cases the vow 'till death us do part' was adhered to as well, though not necessarily because couples loved each other more. Divorce was a stigma, generally regarded as a tragedy for all concerned, and many people chose to soldier on in unhappy marriages rather than face social exclusion. But the Sixties brought changes that shook the bastion of traditional marriage, turning more people towards civil ceremonies, and ended with the Divorce Reform Act opening the floodgates for those who wanted out.

Left *The Fifties had seen two great pirate adventures released in the cinema,* Treasure Island *and* Peter Pan, *and come the Sixties, pirates were as popular as ever, especially when it came to fancy dress. An eye-patch, a head scarf, some tin foil and off you'd go, 'oo-arghing' all the way.*

Above *Magnifying glasses were magic. Not only did they make things bigger, they made things hotter as well. Many a young boy's fascination with fire was fuelled by taking a magnifying glass out in the sun and focusing those burning rays on to a small pile of kindling or some poor, innocent insect.*

If you got lost, which kids often did in those days because parents were more relaxed about leaving them to their own devices, you asked a policeman. He would then take you to the station where you would chat to him respectfully until one or both of your parents turned up to claim you.

The church received a boost from the West Indian immigrant population, who maintained the tradition for regular churchgoing in high numbers while attendance among white Christians gradually fell away. Church choirs and Sunday school were features of many children's lives, though, throughout the decade.

DOWN PETTICOAT LANE
The flamboyant fashions of the Fifties were still popular in the Sixties from a nostalgic point of view. These children, the girls in full petticoats, the boy in white tie and tails like Sinatra, are arriving for an 'old time' dance festival – old time as in the previous decade.

Saddled up

Every girl's dream was to own a pony and more and more girls (and boys) were seeing that dream fulfilled. The Pony Club was no longer the preserve of the upper classes and rich country folk. The growing affluence of the Fifties and early Sixties saw its membership rise as riding became the preferred pastime for a lot of middle-class families.

Turn up at a gymkhana and you would be treated to the sight of countless aspiring young girls desperately trying to get the better of their sullen beasts and cajole them into jumping over a few wooden poles. It was a serious business for those involved, but a hilarious spectacle for the casual observer, and one brilliantly captured in the cartoons of Norman Thelwell. His books, such as *A Leg at Each Corner*, published in 1962, held a mirror up to these poor children and gave them the chance to laugh at the hopelessness of their obsession. Of course, there would always be one girl who got it right and scooped up all the prizes and rosettes.

TWIST AND SHOUT *Streets lined with cars were becoming a common sight and posed an ever-increasing threat to children playing outside. These children are carrying out a daily ritual of dancing the twist in their street in a bid to prevent vehicles from using it and preserve it as the playground it had been for decades.*

In the early Sixties there were 80,000 children living in care. Finding foster families or adoptive parents for them was very difficult as state funding was insufficient. For immigrant children like those in this picture, the likelihood of being boarded out with a family was even more remote.

Children liked to seek their entertainment in groups and organized children's
shows were a familiar and popular feature of seaside towns in holiday season.
Punch and Judy, magic shows and other entertainments kept the kids
amused while their parents enjoyed a few precious moments of time alone.

Without the provision of formal childcare, women who worked had to make their own arrangements for the children. Grandparents were the common solution but even that led to some interesting situations, like this woman picking hops while her grandson sleeps in the trough.

The British knew how to build motorcycles in those days, with names like Royal Enfield, Triumph, Norton and BSA dominating the global market. These boys are admiring a new Panther from Phelon & Moore, one of the last to roll off the Yorkshire production line before the firm closed down in 1966.

POND DIPPING *A net on a stick and an old jam jar were all the tackle you needed to go fishing for minnows or sticklebacks in the local pond. Once you'd got your catch safely into the jar, you would take it home to show mum, who would say, 'I wondered where that jar had gone.'*

Say 'Ahhh'

• •

This boy is actually auditioning for a place in the choir at
Exeter Cathedral but it's not a great advertisement for his
dentist. Teeth in the Sixties were a feature that most people
kept covered up. They were not in a good state. The end of
sugar rationing the previous decade had seen consumption
rise to a tooth-rotting 50kg per person per year and only
five per cent of children at the age of 12 showed no signs of
tooth decay.

Most adults preferred to take their chances, only
going to the dentist when they were in pain, but now
that childrens' dental care was free on the NHS, they did
drag their kids along for a check-up every six months. For
many children this was their worst nightmare, their Room
101. You'd sit in the waiting room, trying to distract yourself
with one of the dog-eared, out-of-date magazines and
block out the sound of the drill coming from down the
corridor. Then you'd be called in, examined and told you
needed ten fillings. Only in later years did you learn that the
dentist was paid by the filling.

FREE SPIRITS *The spirit of liberation for which the Sixties are remembered came from the children of the time. Their natural exuberance and sociability was given a freer rein than in previous decades and their joie de vivre began to rub off on the manner and style of society as a whole.*

Left *Going camping was a highlight for many children in the Sixties. As well as the Boy Scouts and Girl Guides, there were camps organized among schools where you would make new friends and bond with them while learning skills like cooking and talking to girls.*

Above *Crossing the road safely became an important lesson for children but in-car safety was given less consideration. There were no seatbelts in the back and it was often a case of fitting the kids in however you could, as long as you stopped occasionally to let them stretch their legs.*

For many children in the Sixties, your first day at school was your first day away from mum and home, an often traumatic experience but one that quickly passed. There was plenty to take your mind off home,

School Days

such as the sickly bottle of milk you had to drink every day, which always seemed to be either warm or frozen. Either way it was an ordeal to get through, but you had no choice. Discipline was strict and those who misbehaved would get smacked or rapped across the knuckles with a ruler. The routine of reading, writing and arithmetic, taught by a lone teacher with a blackboard and chalk, was broken up by nature trails or Music and Movement classes that were broadcast all round the country through square wooden speakers in the classrooms. Other diversions were the visit of the nit nurse, sight, hearing and colour blindness tests and the polio vaccine given on a sugar lump. And then, at the end of primary school, came the 11+, which determined whether you would go to a grammar school or a secondary modern.

Above *There were no pre-school nurseries to give children a gentle introduction to school; they were thrown in at the deep end as they reached their fifth birthday and expected to swim. Having an older sibling at the same school was always helpful, though not necessarily for the older sibling.*

Right *Listening and moving to music and group singing were regular features of primary education in the Sixties. The School Broadcasting Council would transmit music lessons to schools throughout the country and you would sing along to traditional folk songs or listen to mood music and pretend to be a tree.*

HEALTHY BONES *The daily ⅓ pint of milk was an obligatory part of every child's diet at school. In winter it would freeze and the caretaker would thaw it out by the radiator, making it warm and sour. It also had to be drunk through a straw, thus drawing out the agony.*

Attack!

Secondary schools in the Sixties began to take on the familiar appearance of modern state schools. Indeed, many state schools were built in the Sixties and their particular brand of architecture remains associated with the comprehensive school system, which was fully implemented in 1965. Ugly buildings of brick, metal and glass with tarmac playgrounds fenced in like cages became the backdrop for the new comprehensive school kids, still in uniform but now wearing long trousers. Most schools were still single-sex until the latter part of the decade and the curriculum was gender specific. Girls learnt domestic skills like sewing and cooking, boys learnt woodwork. The nation of shopkeepers was breeding a generation of carpenters and seamstresses. These modern institutions were a lot better equipped than the schools of old but certain uncomfortable traditions remained, such as the use of 'greaseproof' toilet paper, which scratched and offered no absorption whatsoever. Fittingly, each sheet was printed with the instruction: 'Now wash your hands please.' Consequently, most children avoided the toilets at school unless they had an appointment with the school bully.

ROAD SAFETY *With the roads becoming busier all the time, children who rode bicycles were encouraged to develop their road sense and safety awareness in special sessions at school. At the end of the training you would take the Cycling Proficiency Test, which certified you as a safe and capable road user.*

Left *Music and Movement classes encouraged children to express themselves and overcome their feelings of self-consciousness. With instructions broadcast through tinny speakers, you would pretend to be a tree swaying in the wind, or a piece of seaweed perhaps, wafting in the tide.*

Right *PE lessons involved a lot of gymnastics, such as vaults, somersaults, handstands and cartwheels. Building human pyramids was not par for the course but the minimal uniform of shorts and nothing else was. Physical Education was all about the aptitude of the human body. Clothes only got in the way.*

Britain's favourite schoolboy

One of the top entertainers of the time was the diminutive Jimmy Clitheroe, whose radio series *The Clitheroe Kid* ran throughout the Sixties and led to a television show, *Just Jimmy*, which ran from 1964 to 1968. Clitheroe measured only 4 ft 3 in tall and played the part of a mischievous schoolboy. Although he established the role on radio, he would always dress the part when recording each show so as not to let down the live studio audience.

For listeners, the illusion of the naughty schoolboy was vivid and he became one of the country's most successful and highly paid live acts with his catchphrase, 'Don't some mothers 'ave 'em!' When it came to television, however, the fact that Clitheroe was not an 11-year-old boy but a man in his forties became harder to disguise and Clitheroe began to worry that his act might be running out of steam. Like many comedians, his personality off stage was much more serious and guarded. He had an extremely close relationship with his mother and died from an overdose of sleeping pills on the day of her funeral.

Left *Primitive mechanical calculating machines were still around in the mid-Sixties, a complex arrangement of crank handles, pinwheels and sliders that were capable of complex calculations. Electronic calculators did begin to circulate during the Sixties, but it would be a few more years before they would replace the slide rule and the good old pen and paper.*

Above *Smoking began to be recognized as a health risk in the Sixties and most schoolkids would have to go and sneak one in behind the bike sheds, but at this school in Yorkshire, the headmaster allowed senior boys to smoke in a designated smoking room, in the belief that it would remove the mystique.*

Though children were still encouraged to get out and make their own entertainment, there was no shortage of things to keep you amused in the Sixties… but chief among them was a form of entertainment that didn't involve leaving the house: television.

The Things We Did

Having begun the decade with two channels, BBC and ITV, a third, BBC2, was launched in 1964 and two years later the BBC started broadcasting in colour. It was a revelation. Now you could see that Andy Pandy's stripes were blue and white, not grey and white. There were no remote controls, though. You changed channel by turning a dial on the set, so the sensible thing to do was sit right up close where the dial was always in reach. For pre-school children there was *Watch With Mother*, a collection of programmes including Andy Pandy, The Flowerpot Men, Camberwick Green and others, scheduled mid-afternoon so young children could have a sleep after lunch, then wake up and watch 15 minutes of television before 4pm, when *Jackanory* would signal the transition to programmes for schoolchildren, such as *Blue Peter* and *Animal Magic*.

Hold on tight!

• •

Bank holidays often meant a visit to an amusement park.
For decades these places had offered thrills unlike anything
else in life, unless you happened to be a racing driver or
an astronaut. Speed, acceleration, gravity and centrifugal
force could be experienced in extremes on the waltzers,
parachutes, big wheels and roller-coasters, bringing out
the adrenaline junkie in all who rode them – even though
the term adrenaline junkie was yet to be coined. Laughter
and screams filled the air, clashing with the clanging of bells
and music from the merry-go-round and mingling with
the sweet aroma of candyfloss and toffee apples, cigarette
smoke and hotdogs in a mesmerizing maelstrom that dulled
the senses and left everyone walking around with a vacant
grin on their face. Everyone, that is, except the cool lads
in leather jackets with greased hair who manned the rides,
barking orders at people when to get on and get off and
looking out for single girls on the dodgems so they could
jump aboard their car and manfully steer it to safety.

BEAR NECESSITIES

The fortunes of the animals at London Zoo were a regular soap opera in the Sixties, as people flocked to see the star attractions like Guy the gorilla, Goldie the golden eagle and Pipaluk the polar bear. Pipaluk was born in 1967 and was only the second polar bear to be reared at the zoo.

Above *Some days, of course, it rained but that didn't stop people going about their regular business. There was a major flood of the River Severn in 1960, which left much of Gloucester submerged, conjuring up amusing references to Dr Foster, but this milkman continues to carry out his rounds regardless.*

Right *Buster the Corgi gets his daily pinta as his owner milks the cow by hand. If you found yourself on holiday near a farm, you could go and ask the farmer for some fresh milk every day and he might even let you milk the cow yourself.*

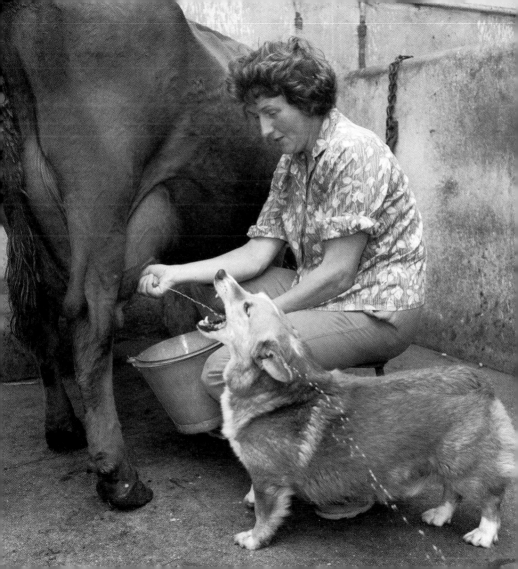

ON THE GRID *Fifteen budding Jim Clarks line up at Crystal Palace race circuit for the start of the pedal-car Grand Prix. Children's toys were becoming a lot more sophisticated but they still required some input on the child's part, in this case a lot of leg work.*

Ice cream!

It was a sound that sent children wild and drove adults to despair: the chimes of the ice cream van arriving in the neighbourhood. Lyons' Mister Softee and Walls' Mr Whippy vans were new to Britain at the start of the decade, but children immediately understood the wonders that they bestowed. Soft ice cream, piped into a cone and topped off with a Cadbury's 99 flake – that was the dream. Or else you'd settle for an ice lolly on a stick. Fabs, Funny Feet and Rockets were always popular. But you had to earn them. The cry of 'Mummy, can I have an ice cream?' would be met by the ingenious response, 'If you ask you don't get.' So you'd try not to ask, while jumping up and down excitedly and casting longing glances in the direction from where the chimes of 'Greensleeves' or 'Popeye the Sailorman' were coming. In summer, ice cream vans began to turn up outside schools at home time, posing a serious threat to road safety and revelling in the annoyance they caused countless mothers.

Britain's last steam passenger train ran in 1968, but those beautiful locomotives would not be lost forever. Steam enthusiasts took over old lines like the Bluebell Line in Sussex and turned them into living museums, where families could go on days out and relive a bygone age.

Britain's historic sites and traditional pageants were popular attractions for family days out. These people are blocking their ears as the cannons fire a 62-gun salute to mark the Queen's birthday at the Tower of London. The boy on the left is wearing a duffel coat, a popular fashion item of the time.

RECLAIM THE STREETS *One solution to the growing danger for children on the roads was this mini town, the Cumberland Community Play Centre in Camden, London, where children were free to ride their bikes and drive their toy cars without any threat from the vehicles of the real world.*

Bouncing back to you

• •

Beach holidays in Britain were all the rage and the early Sixties saw the arrival of a new activity on many of Britain's beaches: the trampoline. Trampolines had been around in some shape or form for several decades, but they weren't commercialized until the American Nissen company developed its own brand of trampoline and set up Nissen UK to market them in Britain. Though the trampolines themselves were made to rigorous safety standards, there were no nets to keep you from bouncing off the side and so accidents were not unusual. Nevertheless, the exhilaration of leaping high in the air above a crowded beach proved a popular draw for the fun-lovers of the Sixties.

In the middle of the decade, Nissen unveiled a variation on the theme, a trampolining game called Spaceball, which it demonstrated at various holiday camps. Spaceball involved a three-dimensional trampoline with a double net down the middle that had a tube running through it. A player bounced up and down on each side of the net, trying to throw a ball through the tube. The game survived late into the 1970s.

Keeping order

• •

Saturday Morning Pictures was a long-standing tradition
by the Sixties. Children aged between about 7 and 13
would go to their local cinema for a morning medley of
cinematic entertainment, and a chance to cause mischief
in the dark. As soon as the doors opened everyone would
surge in, scrambling to get the best seats. Once everyone
had sat down, the lights would go down and the mischief
would commence. Things would be thrown, seats would be
clambered over, jokes would be shouted out. The films did
provide a diversion. First there would be a cartoon, such as
Tom and Jerry or Bugs Bunny, followed by a comedy short,
starring Laurel and Hardy or some other clowns. Then
the lights would go up and the compere, wearing a tuxedo,
would appear along with an organist who rose up through
the stage, and he would lead a sing-song and hand out prizes.
He would usually have a few things thrown at him and would
admonish the culprits, before dimming the lights again for
the main feature. This picture shows boxer Dave Charnley,
the Dartford Destroyer, ensuring order is maintained.

Above *Holidays abroad were now within the budget of many families. Commercial air travel was opening up the world, though for most a holiday abroad meant queuing at the ports to take a ferry over to France and mainland Europe. The British penchant for queuing had found a new arena.*

Right *The lollipop lady became a familiar sight on Britain's roads, helping to ensure safety for children crossing. Most children walked to school and the roads were becoming increasingly dangerous. Lollipop ladies (and men), so called because of their round sign on a stick, were friendly and reassuring faces on your way to school.*

FIRST POSITION *The Rotor was a popular feature at funfairs. People loved the adrenaline rush of defying gravity as the cylinder spun round faster and faster and you were pressed against the wall, the floor gradually dropping away to leave you hanging above it.*

The posher hotels employed page boys straight from school, aged 15, to carry out jobs such as carrying cases and running errands. They dressed in familiar military-style uniforms with pillbox hats, like little drummer boys from the Crimean War, and were part of the pageantry of high-end hotel life.

Adventure holidays in Britain were still popular for young people, who had yet to discover the freedom of gap year tours to Thailand or summer holidays in the Med. A good walk with the girls in one of Britain's beauty spots was enough to clear the mind and invigorate the soul.

The model white-collar family of the Sixties gathers together in the living room, their faces illuminated by the light from the television screen. This somewhat idealized image of family life disguises some of the blemishes that existed behind closed doors but the overriding impression is accurate. Families spent a lot more time together. They ate together, sitting round a dining table, and they often watched television together. Children were expected to play their part in helping to run the home: washing up, vacuuming and helping dad in the garden were all part of normal life. And they did what they were told, with mum usually being the one at home keeping order during the day and dad coming home in the evening to administer punishments to anyone who had misbehaved.

Family entertainment became part of the weekly ritual, with game shows and situation comedies a regular part of Saturday night viewing. Television kept families indoors more than in previous decades but they did go out together too, to the zoo or the seaside or to sporting events.

The Way We Were

HORSEPOWER *Most homes were still heated by coal fires and you got your coal delivered in sacks by the coalman. Along with the rag and bone man, the coalman was one of the last delivery services to use a horse and cart and the sound of those hooves clip-clopping up the road always got you rushing to the window.*

The newly constructed Victoria Line offered commuters in London a much faster journey between Victoria Station and Walthamstow, but lucky was the businessman who got to sip a cup of tea in an empty carriage. You were allowed to smoke on the Tube, though, something which seems unimaginable now.

With only three channels to choose from, popular TV programmes drew huge audiences and were major talking points. People would often watch them together in pubs and social clubs, where they could get a pint of beer for a shilling, rising to two shillings by the end of the decade.

DRIVER'S REST *Owning your own car meant you could pack all your belongings on the roof rack and take it away on holiday. People were discovering that long car journeys were very tiring, so, with no services to call into, they would pull over in some convenient lay-by and stretch their legs, or even take a nap.*

They think it's all over

The Sixties saw the swansong of English football. Having 'given the game to the world' and shown them how to play it, England had spent the years since the war trying to cling on to its status as the father of football, despite growing evidence to the contrary. It had watched its disciples go ahead and play the first three World Cups while it maintained an aloof detachment. Then, having entered in 1950, it had failed to get beyond the quarter-finals on any occasion. Humiliating defeats to Hungary in 1953 and 1954 had shown that English football was no longer at the cutting edge, and so by the time the Sixties came, obituaries were already being written for the birthplace of football. The 1966 World Cup gave England the chance to prove there was life in the old dog yet and, roared on by patriotic crowds, they did just that. Winning the trophy in thrilling style before the Queen at Wembley, England could claim to be the best in the world… for one last time.

Greetings, grapple fans

Professional wrestling was part of the fabric of British society in the Sixties, thanks to the regular television coverage by ITV. The country's second channel had started broadcasting wrestling in the mid-Fifties, but the real boost came in 1965 with the launch of *World of Sport*, ITV's Saturday afternoon sports programme. While the BBC's rival programme, *Grandstand*, showed horse racing, you could turn to ITV for the dulcet tones of commentator Kent Walton, welcoming you to the Fairfield Halls, Croydon, or the Queen's Hall, Preston, or any one of countless municipal baths up and down the country. Wrestling was popular throughout, especially among old ladies, who could be seen in the front row at every bout and were not averse to joining in, attacking the pantomime villains like Mick McManus with their handbags. McManus was one of the biggest stars, along with Shirley 'Big Daddy' Crabtree, Jackie Pallo and others, but you never knew for sure whether their conflicts were stage-managed or for real. They certainly hammed it up for the cameras but the truth of it was, nobody really cared. It was entertainment.

The Pearly way

Pearly Kings and Queens were icons of Cockney London,
their dark suits and hats covered in pearlescent buttons,
and feathers for the Queens, featuring in photographs of
the capital and making occasional television appearances.
Anyone who hadn't been familiar with this quirky tradition
soon became so, learning the story of Henry Croft, the 19th
century orphan boy who swept the streets of Somers Town
market and collected the buttons that fell off the suits of
the costermongers to sew on to a suit of his own. Wearing
his gaudy 'whistle and flute', he began to collect money
for the poor and needy and devoted the rest of his life to
charitable causes. His example inspired others to follow suit
(no pun intended) and by the Sixties every London borough
had its own Pearly King and Queen. They would meet
every month and plan their fundraising campaigns and in
September they would take part in a harvest festival parade
that featured other traditions such as Morris dancing,
marching bands and horse-drawn carts.

Day trippers

The British had been flocking to the seaside for decades, but the growth in private car ownership saw them packing the beaches in vast numbers. Most people were given two weeks' paid holiday a year, so days off were rare and if they happened to coincide with the sun coming out, everybody would jump at the opportunity to get away for some sea air and a change of scene. The drawback was that the scene was not much different from the crowds swarming over London Bridge to work in the City on any given work day, other than the fact that they weren't wearing pinstripe suits and bowler hats. You could sit on the beach at Margate, where this picture was taken, and spend the entire day without ever seeing the sea! But that didn't seem to put the day trippers off. The thing that did was the threat of their chosen resort being invaded by gangs of Mods and Rockers, who terrorized seaside downs from Brighton to Bridlington, waging war on one another in a hooligan echo of Churchill's wartime declaration, 'We will fight them on the beaches.'

RAIN STOPPED PLAY *The Wimbledon Championships were the first event to be broadcast live in colour, with an experimental screen on BBC2 in 1967. The sight of rain was dismal however you viewed it. A year later another milestone was passed when Wimbledon opened up to professional players. Until then it had been restricted to top-ranking amateurs.*

Above *The sight of a man carrying a lifeless body through the streets of London was enough to cause people to stop and stare. In fact, the body is a dummy to be used as a prop for the stage play* Arsenic and Old Lace, *which starred Dame Sybil Thorndike and a 31-year-old Richard Briers.*

Right *Thanks largely to the influence of the BBC, the Proms at the Royal Albert Hall grew greatly in prominence and international stature during the Sixties and attracted big crowds. In 1966 the Moscow Radio Orchestra became the first foreign ensemble to perform, setting the trend for major international performers in years to come.*

ANIMAL MAGIC *Crowds line the railings as two keepers from London Zoo risk their necks trying to recapture a giant coypu. Animal attractions at zoos and safari parks were very popular in the Sixties, when very few people had the chance to see them in their natural habitat and dissenting voices about keeping them captive were rare.*

*The West Indian immigrants who had started coming to Britain
in large numbers since the late 1940s found a passionate link
with their heritage at the cricket. Test matches between England
and the West Indies became vibrant, noisy, fun occasions, far
removed from the genteel traditions of the game.*

Seven years after the Coronation, the people of Britain had another
Royal occasion to celebrate: the marriage of Princess Margaret to Antony
Armstrong-Jones. Despite the rather sad story behind the marriage
(the princess had been forbidden from marrying her true love Peter
Townsend), crowds put out the flags and lined the streets once more.

The Times They Are A-Changin'

Building on the foundations that had been laid in the Fifties, the Sixties brought significant changes to the way we lived. Britain had gone from being a country where people dressed the same, had the same haircuts and followed the same ideals to one where individuality was king. It was a time for self-expression and experimentation, for speaking out and 'dropping out'. The spirit of invention was still rife but with so many frontiers conquered and so many boundaries crossed, it was the exploration of your own mind that captured the youthful imagination. Music, art and fashion all challenged the accepted rules and rock stars made insubordination cool. Society was adjusting its idea of normal. After more than a decade of strategic immigration, Britain had become a multicultural society and was embracing the fact that being British no longer meant being white. Neither did it mean keeping a stiff upper lip and always looking 'respectable'. But there was still a sense of pride in being British and by the end of the decade the nation's gifts to the world had gone supersonic.

Left *The landscape of Britain was changing in the Sixties too, with the building of new trunk roads and motorways, where you really could get a sense of the freedom of the open road. Car ownership had grown rapidly but there was still plenty of room on the roads.*

Above '*King and Queen', a sculpture by Henry Moore, goes on display at the Tate Gallery in London in 1967. Though Moore was an artist of long standing, his work influenced much of the psychedelic art of the late Sixties and helped to change popular appreciation of what was art.*

Proving that Britain could still come up with ingenious inventions, the Hovercraft, developed by Sir Christopher Cockerell, went into use as a form of public transport. This one ferried passengers to and from the Isle of Wight, zipping across the Solent on a cushion of air, so much faster than the ferry.

Not quite as successful as the Hovercraft were the amphibious vehicles that became the obsession of numerous inventors. The dream was to create a car that you could drive into the sea, presumably so that you could take your holidays anywhere in the world.

Tales from the riverbank

Family days out took on an altogether more casual look.
The clothes parents wore were radically different to those
just a decade before. Mums with Jackie Kennedy haircuts
in trousers and T-shirts, dads in round-neck sweaters with
no collar. And the places you went changed too. Now
you could really explore the countryside, without having
to go where the buses and trains went or hike for miles.
You could travel further faster, so it didn't even have to be
a whole day out – you could pop out for the afternoon.
And you could take more with you too: picnic hampers,
deckchairs, bicycles, balls and Frisbees. Just pack them
all in the car and pull right up to your chosen stretch of
riverbank. Easy. Your parents would leave you to run off and
play, climbing trees and playing war, only coming back when
it was picnic time. On the way home you might stop at a
pub, the grown-ups would go in and you'd be brought out
a fizzy drink and a packet of crisps to have in the car.

Supersonic

In 1969 all eyes were on the moon and the historic mission that saw Neil Armstrong take that small step for the first time, but in Britain we had our own reason for watching the skies. Concorde, the first supersonic passenger jet, made its maiden test flight that year. Though it would be another seven years before it was ready to start carrying commercial passengers, excitement over the plane was contagious. On a practical level it would cut the flight time to New York in half, but most Concorde enthusiasts weren't interested in that. Few of them would ever get to fly in it but that didn't matter – this was a plane that was better from the outside than the inside. Those early flights gave the public a taste of the sheer, visceral thrill to be had when seeing that sleek form gliding across the sky, preceded by a distinctive rumble that could only come from Concorde's engines. Though it remained an exclusive mode of transport for the privileged few, its drop nose and delta wings became a symbol of British (and French) engineering excellence.

One attempt at innovation that didn't catch on was this conveyor belt, designed to serve and take away dinner plates. It was never considered a worthy replacement for a good team of waiting staff and the idea of delivering food on a conveyor belt had already been developed in Japan.

The British appeared to have two obsessions: inventions and cars. Here's one that combined the two: a Trotent – for the camper who insists on sleeping with his car. The advantages over a conventional tent pitched next to your car were hard to see, and it failed to capture the public imagination.

Behind bars

The exploration of the human mind brought out the more eccentric side of the British personality in the Sixties. In a scene that could have been conjured up by the Monty Python team – who began to act out their own absurd parody of Britain's eccentricities in 1969 – three art students take up residence in a bear cage at Chessington Zoo so that they can observe people's reactions. The general reaction was to ask, 'Have they gone stark raving mad?' and to brand them as 'bonkers', but in terms of anthropological experiments involving people trying to lead day-to-day lives in captivity while the rest of society looked on, they were years ahead of their time. And indeed they did attract the same sort of fascination that Big Brother would do more than 30 years later.

It's worth noting that Chessington was a zoo in the Sixties, with animals and everything. The World of Adventures would come years later, when people had grown tired of watching bored animals doing nothing but read the paper.

STONED *A group of young fans watch the Rolling Stones in concert at Wimbledon Palais. Pop music was catching kids at a younger and younger age, thanks to TV shows like* Top of the Pops, *which first aired in 1964. The sheer thrill of seeing their heroes in the flesh drove fans into an uncontrollable frenzy.*

FASHION CENTRE *British fashion set the trend around the world in the Sixties and the place everyone flocked to was Carnaby Street. This unassuming little shopping street just off Regent Street became the shop window for the trendiest designers, most notably Mary Quant, and consequently the cool place for models and rock stars to be seen.*

Beatlemania

If there was one group that owned the Sixties it was The Beatles. Their career spanned the decade almost to the day – forming at the start of the 1960s, disbanding in the spring of 1970 – and their development from jobbing rock'n'roll band to pioneers of psychedelia and musical experimentation reflected, and to a large degree inspired, the changing face of society during that time. The public at large got their first taste of The Beatles with the release of their debut single, 'Love Me Do', in 1962, soon followed by their first appearance on television. Their next single, 'Please Please Me', went to the top of the charts. The Beatles had truly arrived. The rest of the decade would see them make 12 albums, star in five films, conquer America, disappear to India, be awarded the MBE and, in the case of John Lennon, hand it back again. Their career was shorter than that of many bands who have had a fraction of the impact and it was all played out against the ever-changing backdrop of the Sixties.

PLEASE
QUEUE
ON
OTHER SIDE
OF THIS BOARD
FOR
THE
BEATLES
CONCERT TICKETS.
BOOKING OFFICE OPEN

WE ARE THE MODS With their distinctive uniform of parka coats, pork pie hats, Chelsea boots and Italian scooters, a gang of Mods attracts the attentions of the local constabulary in Clacton-on-Sea. Riding without a crash helmet was not illegal, but picking fights with Rockers and terrorizing innocent holidaymakers was.

MY GENERATION *After The Beatles and the Stones, The Who were the next biggest thing in British rock music, striking an attitude of youthful rebellion that surpassed that of any other group and encapsulating the mood of the time with the ironically immortal lyric, 'Hope I die before I get old'.*

Peace and love, man!

• •

1967 was the Summer of Love, when the youth culture everyone was talking about was 'hippies'. The hippies were the natural extension of the steady rejection of traditional values that had been taking place among the young generation since the early 1950s. Whereas previous youth movements had challenged these values, the hippies disregarded them altogether. Marriage, fidelity, consumerism, materialism, war… they saw no need for any of these things, preferring to live for the moment, make love not war and, in some cases, explore the universe within through the use of mind-altering drugs.

For most kids, however, while the principles of peace and love were indisputable, there were serious impracticalities about the hippie doctrine. To be a proper hippie, it seemed, you either had to be independently wealthy or you had to drop out altogether. So they followed the most fundamental hippie mantra of all and did their own thing: they wore the clothes, listened to the music and went to the festivals, but from Monday to Friday they carried on with their work or studies as normal.

Left *The Isle of Wight Festival brought the decade to a close in far out style for Britain's youth. Attendance grew from 15,000 in 1968 to over 200,000 the following year, due largely to the appearance of Bob Dylan. There was one more, even bigger, festival in 1970, before Parliament put a stop to it.*

Right *The decade had begun with jukeboxes and rock'n'roll dancing. By the end these things were anachronisms, styles from a bygone age, museum pieces kept alive by nostalgia junkies, while mainstream music moved on into heavy rock or pop and dancing became a free-form expression that you made up on the spur of the moment.*

IN WITH THE NEW

Concorde appears in the sky over Nelson's Column, a symbol of new Britain frozen in time against an icon from its imperial past. The Sixties had ushered Britain into the modern age: the country was less powerful, less disciplined, less grand, but more inclusive, more broad-minded and still capable of making a big noise.